Manager

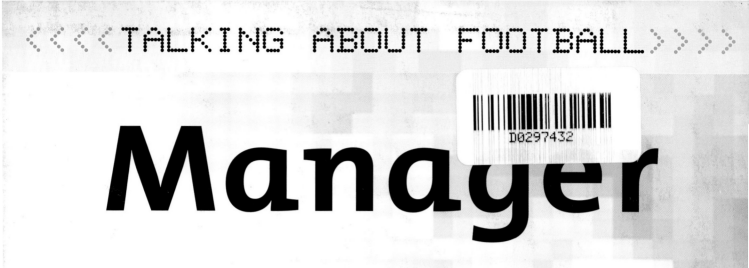

Antony Lishak

W
FRANKLIN WATTS
LONDON • SYDNEY

First published in 2006 by
Franklin Watts
338 Euston Road
London NW1 3BH

Franklin Watts Australia
Hachette Children's Books
Level 17/207 Kent Street
Sydney NSW 2000

© 2006 Franklin Watts

Editor: Adrian Cole
Art Director: Jonathan Hair
Design: Matthew Lilly
Cover and design concept:
Peter Scoulding

Photograph credits:
John Babb/Pro Sport/Topfoto: 13, 25. Geoff
Caddick/Topfoto: 15. Jason Cairnduff/Pro
Sport/Topfoto: 21. Gareth Copely/PA/Topfoto: 14.
Empics/Topfoto: cover, 3, 4, 6, 8,10,11,16,19, 22, 23,
24, 26. Richard Heathcote/Star Images/Topfoto:
12. Tommy Hindley/Pro Sport/Topfoto: 9, 17, 18,
20. PA/Topfoto: 7, 27.

A CIP catalogue record for this book is
available from the British Library.

Dewey classification: 796.334'069

ISBN-10: 0-7496-6508-4
ISBN-13: 978-0-7496-6508-1

Printed in China

Franklin Watts is a division of Hachette Children's Books.

Contents

⚽ Club staff

Football is a team sport, but someone has to bring all the players and staff together. The manager is in charge of the football team. He or she organises the team so the players perform well.

> " If the players want to win the World Cup they have to score goals, they have to work, they have to run, they have to give everything. "
>
> – Luiz Felipe Scolari, international manager

▷ Otto Rehhagel (left), manager of Greece's national team, celebrates victory in the 2004 European Championship.

⚠️ Managers are helped and supported by other staff members.

The back room staff

The manager of a football team is helped by lots of other members of staff. They are rarely noticed by the fans and are often called 'the backroom staff' because they work behind the scenes.

- The **manager** organises all the staff, including the players and the backroom staff. He or she chooses the team for each game, travels with the players to all the football matches, and makes decisions during the game that change the team formation and tactics. Some managers play for the team too. They are called player-managers.

Back room staff

- The **first team coach** works with the manager, helping the players to learn the manager's tactics and to play well.

- The **youth coach** helps to train the younger, less-experienced players of the club to improve their football skills.

- The **fitness coach** helps to keep the squad fit and healthy. He or she plans meals for the players and makes training programmes for them to follow.

- **Positional specialists** help develop specific skills, for example, most teams have a specialist goalkeeping coach.

- The **physiotherapist** (sometimes called the physio) treats injured players on and off the pitch. He or she works closely with the fitness coach to keep the players fit.

⚽ Team training

Fans only see players in action on the pitch, but it takes a lot to get the players ready. They train hard almost every day. The manager makes sure that all the players are fully prepared.

> In football you have to concentrate on the whole team, not just individuals.
>
> – Bobby Robson, former England manager

▷ A manager instructs his players during training in the gym. Fitness coaches make training programmes that help to keep the players fit.

In the gym

The manager and the fitness coach work out training programmes for the players, and keep a close watch on them as they exercise. The players have their breathing and heart rates checked to ensure they are ready to play.

On the practice pitch

Most of a footballer's week is spent at the training ground. Here managers use their coaching skills. They help each player to work as part of the team. The manager and the first team coach plan special routines that the team can put into practice during a match.

 Manager Jose Mourinho (centre) watches over his squad at their training ground.

SKILLS TIPS

- Always listen to your manager or coach when he or she is explaining tactics to the team. You will be expected to carry out the instructions on the pitch.
- Always tell your manager if you do not understand something that is being explained to you.

Talking tactics

The manager, with help from his or her staff, plans the best way to beat the opposition. This is called working out tactics. It is important that the team is aware of the strengths and weakness of the opposition. For example, if the opposing team has a good striker, the manager may work out a plan for two defenders to put pressure on him or her by staying close.

⚽ Match preparations

While the players are training or resting, the manager and coaching staff also spend their time planning for the match.

Team scout John Bond (left) watches players closely during a football game. He makes a note of how the team play, and any weaknesses they may have.

Scouts

To prepare for a game the manager has to collect information about the opponents. If possible, the manager watches them play and takes notes. Most managers also have a team of experts, called scouts, who they send to watch games and then report back.

Studying videos

Many football games are on the TV and managers can watch lots of recorded highlights of their opponent's games. They can fast-forward and freeze the game to show important parts of it to their players.

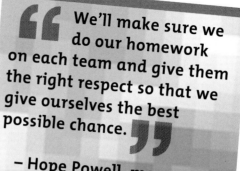

We'll make sure we do our homework on each team and give them the right respect so that we give ourselves the best possible chance.

– Hope Powell, manager of the England women's team

▷ Managers bring all the information together. Then they talk through a plan with their players, so they all know what to do during the game.

Picking the team

Managers choose 11 players from those available in their squad. They make a decision to choose players based on their fitness and who is playing well. Managers also have to choose 5 substitute players, but only 3 can be used during the game.

⚽ Match day

Managers have a routine for match days. This helps the players to get ready by kick-off time. The build-up can take about three hours. Each player must eat the right things at the right time and warm up properly.

> ### ▷ HALL OF FAME
>
> Hassan Shehata managed Egypt to a record fifth triumph in the African Cup of Nations in 2006, having coached the youth team to victory at the 2003 African Youth Championship. He is well known for his ability to make good tactical changes.

⚠ Managers give team talks to their players before, during and after the game.

When and where is the game?

A match could start in the morning, afternoon or evening, so it is important that the build-up routine is timed carefully. Home games are easier to prepare for than away games, when the team may have to travel a long distance to get to their opponent's stadium.

Touchline pressure

During a game some managers call out instructions from the technical area in front of the team bench. Others sit quietly and talk to their staff. Managers rarely make team changes during the first half. They prefer to wait until half time to see if their tactics are working.

> A [manager] may be 60% responsible for a team's performance in the build-up to a match, but once the game has begun he is less than 10% accountable for what happens on the pitch.
>
> – Cesar Luis Menotti, Argentina's 1978 World Cup-winning manager

⚠ During a game players and the team staff wait on the bench. All they can do is watch the game and play their part when the time comes.

Substitutes

During the second half, managers sometimes make tactical changes. These will depend on how well the team is playing. Managers also swap injured or tired players for substitute players. These players wait on the substitutes' bench until they are needed.

The final whistle

Win, lose or draw, when the final whistle blows the game is over. If things have gone well, it is an opportunity to praise the team. If things have gone badly, it is a chance to assess what went wrong.

> **Winning breeds confidence and confidence is the most important [thing] in football.**
>
> – Chris Sherrard, journalist

Manager David O'Leary shakes hands with the opposing manager after a no-score draw. It is important for both managers to show respect.

Showing respect

Managers of both teams usually shake hands with each other when the game ends. Being a manager is a very public job, with everybody watching all the time. It is important to set a good example to others.

Post-match interviews

Most managers of top league clubs are asked to give their opinions on the match to television cameras straight after the game. Sometimes this is difficult if their team lost, but most managers are experienced enough to stay calm.

▽

Jose Mourinho and a crowd of sports photographers and journalists. After an important game managers are often the first people to give an interview.

> I wouldn't say I was the best manager in the business. But I was in the top one.
>
> – Brian Clough, former manager of Nottingham Forest and Derby County

In the changing room

Most managers talk to the team after the game. They keep their post-match comments very brief because the players are tired. The players have showers and get changed. It is important that medical staff treat any injuries to prevent any serious damage.

⚽ Homework

No matter how well the side has played, all managers want their team to play better. They try to learn from their mistakes. The most successful managers always want their team to play perfectly.

▷ Manager Sam Allardyce watches his team from the stands to see how the players perform. He talks to his coach using his ear radio.

No time off

Many clubs record each game on their own cameras. It is quite common for a manager to go home to watch the game again. Some clubs have people whose job it is to collect information about each player's performance during the game.

Be prepared!

It is important that the manager has a good overview of what worked and what went wrong during a game. With this information he or she can help each player to identify where they can improve.

▷ HALL OF FAME

Arsene Wenger is Arsenal's most successful manager, winning three premiership titles and four FA Cup finals. His approach helped transform the way most top British clubs trained. In 2004, he became the first manager for over 100 years to lead a team through a season unbeaten. He has been voted Manager of the Year three times.

Dealing with pressure

It takes a very special type of person to become a successful manager. The hopes and dreams of thousands of fans rest upon the success of their team. This puts a lot of pressure on managers, but they know it is part of the job.

“ Some people think football is a matter of life and death...I can assure them it is much more serious than that. ”

– Bill Shankly, former Liverpool manager

⚽ Youth policy

While most of a manager's time is spent preparing the top players for the next game, it is also important to prepare for the future. All clubs have a range of squads, including one for youth players.

> **"** We are a very young team, so we'll need the crowd behind us. **"**
>
> – Jurgen Klinsmann, Germany's World Cup 2006 manager

◁ Jerome Thomas (right) played on the Arsenal Youth Team before training with the first team.

Youth scouts

Managers do not have the time to watch hundreds of under-17s football games. Each club has a group of scouts who spot young talent. If they find promising young players they may ask them to come to the club for a trial.

⚠ Wayne Rooney shoots at the goal during his first game for England. He first played in the youth team at Everton Football Club.

Youth players

Most players spend about three years in the youth squad practising their skills, improving their fitness levels and playing in youth team games. They are watched closely by the youth coach, who reports to the manager. When the manager thinks they are good enough, some young players get a chance to train with the first team. They may even get into the first team squad.

❝ Research has shown that to have a chance of being a footballer, a violinist or whatever at the top level, you need to put in 10,000 hours of practice. Minimum. ❞

— Sam Allardyce, manager

⚽ The transfer market

It takes time for a young player to progress to the first team, so managers buy top players to make a strong squad. Some clubs have lots of money and can buy expensive, highly skilled players.

Improving the team

The manager makes sure that the team has lots of good players, but even the best team could be improved. A manager and his or her scouts always watch for new players who could strengthen the squad.

> " I know everybody is very excited, Edgar is a big player and the one we wanted. Our young players will learn from him. "
>
> – Martin Jol discusses Edgar Davids's transfer from Barcelona to Tottenham Hotspur

Players are bought and sold by clubs on the transfer market. This usually happens between the football seasons.

◁ Martin Jol (left) shows off his new signing Edgar Davids in 2005. Press events like this are proud moments for a manager.

Alex Ferguson has been a manager for over 30 years. After a successful career in Scotland, he moved to Manchester United in 1986 winning eight League championships, five FA Cups and the European Champions League – more trophies than any other manager in English football.

Buying and selling

Managers can buy talented young players from other clubs who they think could develop to be great. Players like these cost less money, but will need more coaching. Sometimes managers sell top players on their team for lots of money. They might use the money to buy two or three new players.

The Manchester United substitutes' bench. Sometimes players who are regularly left out of the team ask to be transferred to another club. They hope to have the chance to play more games.

> The transfer market has changed. In the whole of Europe [in 2005] there were only five transfers in excess of £10 million if you exclude Chelsea.
>
> – David Gill, Chief Executive at Manchester United

Staying up-to-date

Even the most successful managers do not stop learning about the game. They know their team can only stay successful if they can compete with the best sides in other countries.

New backroom ideas

Managers are always looking for ways to improve their player's preparation for games. In recent years some managers have employed 'sports psychologists'. They help players prepare mentally for games.

> A successful [manager] should always be open to new ideas and want to improve their individual skills and knowledge of the game.
> – www.thefa.com

Hernan Crespo receives some physio treatment before training. This is just one way a manager's staff can help to maintain players' performances.

Talking to other managers

Although football is a very competitive sport, it is common for managers and coaches to exchange ideas. Some managers develop close friendships and learn to respect each other's opinions.

▷ Manager Carolina Morace directs her team during a game. Many female managers have brought new ideas to the game.

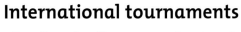

International tournaments

The football season lasts about ten months, but that does not mean that a manager spends two months relaxing on a beach. Major tournaments, such as the World Cup, provide a great opportunity to watch the best players in the world.

⚽ National manager

Top managers want to work at the highest level – and you do not get any higher than international football. It is different from being a club manager and it does not appeal to everyone.

Building the squad

International managers choose the best players from a specific country to join their squad. International teams do not play many games each year. Preparation time is very limited because clubs want their players to be away only for a short time.

▽

Hope Powell is the manager of the England women's team. She led the team to the European Championship 2005 finals.

▷ HALL OF FAME

In 1998, Hope Powell became the first ever full-time manager to be appointed to the England women's team. In her playing days she scored 35 goals in 66 games for the national side. In 2003, she became the first woman to achieve the "UEFA Pro Licence" – the highest coaching award available.

Bruno Metsu signals to his players. The Frenchman became the manager of the Senegal national team in 2000, leading them to their first World Cup Finals in 2002.

High pressure

International managers have to cope with the hopes of fans from an entire country. They also have to be calm, especially when things go badly. It is probably the hardest job in football – but managing a national team to victory in a major competition will guarantee a place in that country's sporting history forever.

> It is not easy to be the [manager] of a national side. It was only when I was doing the job that I realised how difficult it can be, and how it is about more than football.
>
> – Aimé Jacquet, France's 1998 World Cup-winning manager

All about winning

Managers know that if their team does not play well they will become the focus of unhappy fans. If the team loses too many games, they may even get the sack. In the end, they must win.

Getting points

Managers organise their teams in different ways to get good results. This is called their management style. Club team managers do everything they can to win games so the team wins points. Without points the team will stay at the bottom of the league.

> Nothing gives emotions as strong as football. To win a game of football remains top of the top.
>
> – Arsene Wenger, manager

◁ Otto Rehhagel celebrates Greece's win in the European Championship 2004 final. Every manager aims to lead their team to victory.

Who is in charge?

Although the club manager is the person who makes all the important team decisions, he or she is employed by the owners of the football club. All clubs have a 'chairperson' who decides whether the manager is doing a good job. The chairperson may sack the manager if he or she is not successful.

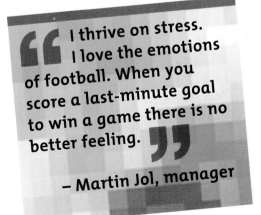

▷ Manager Alex Ferguson applauds the team's fans. Managers know that they have a responsibility to make the club successful.

Just a game

Football is very important for millions of people, and fans can get very excited or upset. However, every manager knows that football is a game that players and fans should enjoy through the good and bad times.

> " I thrive on stress. I love the emotions of football. When you score a last-minute goal to win a game there is no better feeling. "
>
> – Martin Jol, manager

⚽ Websites

http://www.bettersoccermorefun.com
A website full of useful and interesting coaching tips and tactics.

http://www.womenssoccerscene.co.uk
This website focuses on women's and girl's football. It includes the latest game results and football news from the UK.

http://www.footballaustralia.com.au
Website of the Football Federation of Australia, featuring news on the national men's and women's teams. It also includes sections on coaching and football rules, and has weblinks to other Australian-based websites.

http://www.uefa.com
The official website of UEFA, the organisation which runs football in Europe, including the Champions League.

http://www.footballasia.com
This website includes information about all the Asian football competitions, including ones for women.

http://www.fifa.com
Official website of the Fédération Internationale de Football Association. It features football news and history.

http://www.footy4kids.co.uk/
This website has lots of information about training and coaching. There are football drills, practice tips, news articles and a section about football history.

http://www.footballdatabase.com/site/home/index.php
A website packed with details on famous players, managers and competitions. A good place to head to find scoring records of famous strikers.

⚽ Glossary

Advice
– an opinion about what should be done.

Champions League
– the European competition which includes only the best teams from selected European countries.

Competitive
– when two sides are equally matched.

Experience
– knowledge acquired over many years.

First team
– the players chosen regularly by the manager to play in league or competition games.

Football season
– the months in the year when football is played.

Formation
– the way the players are arranged on the pitch.

Highlights
– the most exiting events in a game.

Journalist
– a person who reports on football for the television or newspapers.

Kick off
– when a football game starts.

Organise
– put into practice a particular system.

Pressure
– the feeling of stress at times of crisis.

Programme
– in this sense, a set routine including lots of different elements.

Respect
– to be polite to someone.

Sack, the
– when someone loses their job.

Squad
– all the club's professional players, from which the manager chooses a team.

Stadium
– the large building where football matches are played.

Substitute
– a player who is waiting in reserve to be brought on during a match.

Tactics
– the different ways a team's players are told to play by their coach or manager to beat the other team.

Technical area
– the box marked on the side of the pitch where managers and other staff are allowed to stand.

Transfer
– when a player is bought or sold by a club.

Trial
– a series of practical football tests that show a player's skills.

Index